The Crummy War of Henrietta Eloise Parsons Age 9

Dedicated to Freeling RSL, which honours the veterans who served in The Great War, The Second World War, and every other war; and those marvellous people in the armed services peace-keeping forces. Special thanks to Garry Shearing for his time and invaluable information. To his wife, Annie Shearing, and Cindy Kotek who embody the true spirit of community.

Linda Ruth Brooks

Special thanks to the authors of *Horses, Harrows and Haystacks,* and the Freeling Women's Agricultural Bureau that faithfully recorded and collated that book, along with support for the community.

Copyright © Linda Ruth Brooks 2018

All rights reserved. Without limiting the rights under copyright reserved above, no part of this work/publication may be reproduced, stored in or introduced into a retrieval system, or transmitted, in any form or by any means (electronic, mechanical, print, photocopying, recording or otherwise), without the prior written permission of the copyright owner.

Cover & Interior Design by Linda Brooks

A copy of this book can be found in the National Library of Australia.

ISBN-: 9780648407744

Linda Brooks lives in Adelaide. She gained the attention of a publisher when her short stories found critical acclaim on the ABC website, 'The Making of Modern Australia' and her first published book resulted, *A Curious & Inelegant Childhood*, a memoir of growing up in rural Australia. Linda has written and illustrated children's books, fiction and poetry. Linda's short stories have been published in numerous anthologies: Coastlines 5 & 6 (Southern Cross University), Wood, Bricks & Stone (Catchfire Press) and Grieve (Hunter Writer's Centre) and Longing for Solitude (Stringybark Press). She has won creative writing awards, including first prize for The Legacy University Level Creative Writing Award and first prize for the Gabe Reynaud Creative Writing Award, and the Mater Misericordiae Grieve Writing Award. Linda's books feature her skill as an artist and illustrator.

Fiction/juvenile/military/family

The Crummy War of Henrietta Eloise Parsons Age 9 is a work of fiction. Any similarity between the characters in this book and real people, living or dead, is coincidental. This book, and others by Linda, can be purchased through online bookstores, retail outlets and **http://www.amazon.com**

Introduction

Henrietta (Ellie) Eloise Parsons was minding her own business when The Great War started—going to school, wishing she'd been born a princess, planning parties and eavesdropping on her parents' conversation, like most girls her age.

Her story begins in an unlikely place on an ordinary day, on the other side of the world. It began on a street in Sarajevo in Serbia.

Archduke Franz Ferdinand of Austria, heir to the throne of Austria-Hungary, along with his wife Sophie, was shot and killed by a Serbian rebel on 28 June 1914. Three children were orphaned that day. The eldest, Princess Sophie von Hohenberg was thirteen years old and being a princess was the last thing on her mind, for she dearly loved her Mama and Papa.

The day that began as any other day brought a war that changed history, toppled thrones and empires and had map makers busy redrawing the borders of many European countries.

Then, like a schoolyard brawl, with friend calling on friend to take sides, countries joined in until the world was involved, on one side or the other.

Henrietta was far from the killing fields of war, in the small Australian country town of Freeling, staying with her grandparents, Bill and Helena Kent. She had been sent there from Sydney for the duration of the war by her parents, Frances and James Parsons. Many mothers and fathers living in large cities sent their children to stay with relatives who lived in the country, away from harm.

The Crummy War of Henrietta Eloise Parsons was called The Great War, mainly because no one could believe there'd ever be another war like that one.

They were wrong. There were many more to come, more wars, more killing fields. Then, The Great War, also known as The War to End All Wars, became known as The First World War or World War I.

oOo

On the other side of the world from Henrietta Eloise Parsons, another young girl, Sophie Marie Franziska Antonia Ignatia Alberta von Hohenberg was about to turn 14 years of age. She had just received the news that her beloved Mama and Papa had been shot dead on a city street in Bosnia.

Sophie's father, Archduke Franz Ferdinand had been on an official visit to Sarajevo, in Bosnia. The Archduke shouldn't have been on that street at that time. His driver had taken a wrong turn. The assassin, Gavril Princip, was sitting in a cafe and couldn't believe his luck when the Archduke's car slowed down right in front of him. He ran onto the street and fired two shots, killing both the Archduke and his wife, Sophie.

Henrietta Eloise Parsons was not a fan of History. All those dead kings and dates to remember. Heads being lopped off for any old reason. Who did this and who did that. She lived in Sydney, Australia. Australia had borders where it didn't matter when you crossed one because you were still in the same country.

To Henrietta, History was as boring as trying to play chess with her father. Father's efforts to teach Henrietta how to play chess had ended in disaster when Henrietta had crossed her arms and asked who had decided that the king was worth more than the queen and why the pawns were worth least of all.

If she'd only known it, Henrietta was closer to the truth that underlies History than she realised. And the Crummy War of Henrietta Eloise Parsons, known as The Great War would see many of the world's pawns revolting over precisely that principle. Why should kings, kaisers and tsars have so much more than the workers? Especially ones who sat in rooms called war offices, with models of countries laid out on big tables, with their mountains and valleys, rivers and railways, theatres and parks, towns and homes—and while there, planned movements of troops, ships, planes and artillery to steal places and people that didn't belong to them.

They didn't realise you can't own people, but they were soon going to learn exactly that. And they weren't going to like it.

oOo

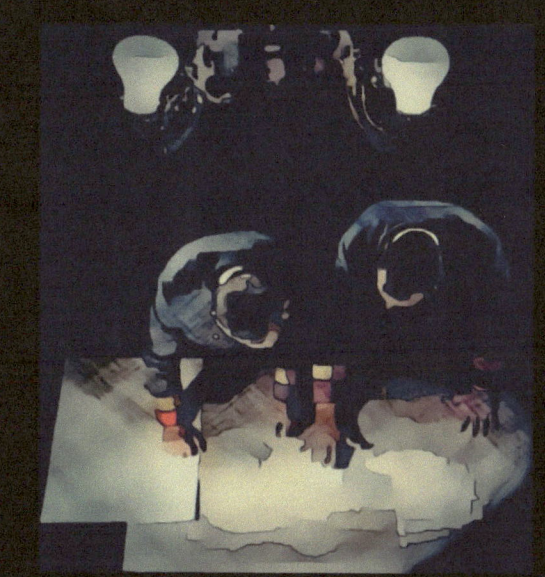

No such thing as too much news

Sydney, Australia, April 1914

There were two different worlds at our house. There was the world of cigars, whisky and politics in my father's domain—the dining room; and the world of committees, high teas and gossip in the sitting room with my mother. As an only child I floated between the two as I pleased, although I preferred my father's company unless the room was crowded with old men and thick with smoke.

My friends' fathers read them bedtime stories but Father read to me from the paper. A senior editor at the *Sydney Morning Herald,* he was determined I would be an educated female. Mother was just as determined that I'd take my place in society, and be like her, which I thought I would. Mother's parties had delicious sandwiches; the women wore wonderful dresses and I never entirely understood what Father was reading.

One night he read about 'a double dissolution of Federal Parliament'. His explanation was so boring I yawned. Mother came in and told him he was taxing my brain. I said that I was fascinated and thinking of going into politics. (I really shouldn't have goaded Mother—I was hoping for a big party for my tenth birthday that year).

Declaring an interest in politics set Mother off about Aunt Bea, Father's younger sister, who wore trousers and rode a motorcycle. Mother was terrified I'd take after Aunt Bea so she hardly ever invited her around, certainly not to one of her precious high teas in the downstairs dining room with its chandeliers and society ladies.

I adored Aunt Bea. She'd laughed when I asked her if she'd taken her place in society. 'Hardly, darling,' she said, 'society wouldn't have me'. She'd been to all kinds of places and had amazing adventures. She'd watched Harry Houdini fly his plane at Randwick Racecourse.

Everything is fine in the Empire

Sydney, Australia, May 1914

Father glared at the newspaper, ignored his breakfast and said, 'I can hear the drums of war rumbling'.'

'What do you mean, Dad?'

Asking was a waste of time because Father mumbled behind his newspaper. Something along the usual lines that certain things weren't meant for the ears of children.

'If it's not for the ears of children then why do you talk about it only a yard from my ears?' I stepped forward to a spot that was close to one yard. I'd been learning about measurement at school.

That was a mistake. Father was far too loud that close to anyone's ears when he yelled. 'Don't give cheek, Henrietta!'

'Don't talk nonsense to your daughter, James. Drums of war indeed! You know she has an overactive imagination. Everything is fine in the Empire.'

'What do you know about Empires, Mum?' I asked. There were a lot of Empires to keep track of.

Another mistake. 'Mind your manners, young lady!' Father boomed.

'If I'm a young lady then you needn't bother so much about what I hear,' I said, retreating to the other side of the room.

'What are they teaching this kid at school, Frances?'

Mother scowled at Father.

'Really, James. Don't ask such disobliging questions over breakfast.'

'What's disobliging mean?' I asked, always willing to learn.

'Rude,' said Father. 'Your mother is accusing me of being rude.'

'James!' Mother put down the fork she was using to move scrambled egg around her plate in slow circles.

This was a sure sign an argument was about to start.

Knowing I would be sent out of the room at any minute, I climbed under the table, a trick I'd discovered so early in life I couldn't remember its beginning.

Some children, of course, don't like their parents arguing, especially if there's anger. My parents, however, rarely became truly cross. For one thing they were hardly ever at home at the same time. This meant I was always hungry for their conversation, but they had a firm rule about not arguing in front of children, so hiding under the table worked well.

If I scampered under the table and wriggled to the middle I could overhear a good many things not intended for my hearing. Keeping perfectly still was always a trial and Father could be a bit long-winded at times, depending on the subject of politics or war. The fact that Mother liked damask tablecloths that nearly touched the floor made hiding easy. Unless I sneezed.

That morning the argument lasted no more than a minute.

I heard a *thud thud* on the table, then Mother's chair scraping as she said, 'James, I will not stay while you stab at the newspaper in that disagreeable fashion.'

There was a light tap-tapping overhead, as Mother added, 'This word here is wrong surely—"susceptible". It couldn't have been you who edited this piece. It sounds like the Archduke was worrying about the contracting the flu, rather than being aware of sensitivities of the Serbs.'

Then she left the room, delivering a few words in a cold voice designed to wound any man who was Senior Editor of the *Sydney Morning Herald*. 'Waste of a penny, that rag.'

'Never heard the like,' Father said. 'A man's better off on his bloody own.' He snapped the paper. 'Everything's fine with the Empire—never heard such rot.'

Austria-Hungary's very bad day

June 30, 1914

Father read several newspapers on the morning of June 30, not just to me, but to Mother as well. I wondered why, but when he began to read about Archduke Franz Ferdinand of Austria-Hungary, I sat up straight and listened.

Father's face was grey as he read—"The Assassin's Victims"—'Prinzip, a Servian student dashed forward, and fired two shots from a Browning pistol. The first hit the Duchess on the right side of her body. The second struck the Archduke in the throat...'

Father stopped there, looked sadly at me and cleared his throat noisily.

Mother sat perfectly still, her eyes wet with tears. 'Oh, James, how positively awful.'

'Father, is that Princess Sophie's parents? The Princess Sophie that has the same birthday as me? Princess Sophie de Hohenberg?'

Father nodded and I sobbed. I knew all the royal princesses in all the countries of Europe, but I adored Princess Sophie best of all. I was upset to hear that she was an orphan. I remembered a rare time when Grandmamma Helena came to visit and told me that I looked like Sophie so I had claimed her as my princess.

I forgot about birthdays. I didn't hear the rest of the words. I just stared at the photograph of Princess Sophie in the newspaper. What use was it being a royal princess for Sophie now?

When Father finished reading, he said quietly, 'This will mean war'.

The papers seemed to share Father's mood about war.

I started talking about newspapers and war at school in History, but the teacher got really uncomfortable and said, 'Hm, ah, well, now that's interesting'.

I came to understand that the word interesting in certain situations was a grownup excuse to get out of saying what they really meant.

Too close to home

August 1914.

Father started reading *all* the newspapers, not just the *Herald*.

Mother said he was obsessed with them. He talked about rumblings of war in Europe. His study was often filled with serious men in dark suits, discussing the Europe situation until late at night. Mother started shooing Father out of the dining room with his guests telling him to make do with cake and cold tea as she wasn't keeping poor Cook up all hours for their grim ramblings.

There was no more talk of birthday parties. The house became busier and quieter. The servants were all on edge. Mother had been talking about changes to the staff. Father had been delighted to let his driver go. According to Mother he'd been longing to return to his carefree youth when he motored all over town.

Father wished he could have gone with Jeffery as his driver was now busily serving all kinds of important government officials and military personnel. Father was pale and tired. He didn't read the papers aloud at breakfast. He didn't read to me at night. He just pecked me on the top of my head, called me his poppet and told me to be a good girl.

Even though he read the paper to himself most of the time, he told us war had been declared on August 4 and we were 'in it with the Brits'. The next morning over breakfast, he said the first shots had been fired, not in Europe but near Melbourne. A German cargo ship had desperately tried to leave Australian waters. Then he said, 'Bloody hell'.

'What on earth does this mean, James?' Mother sat on the edge of her chair in the dining room, waiting for Father to answer. 'That's so close. The war isn't on the other side of the world. This was in Victoria, James. Victoria!'

Father scraped his chair closer to Mother and patted her knee. She twisted her gloves in her hands, like Daisy does when she is wringing out the wet clothes that have been washed.

It will all be over by Christmas

December, 1914

'I hate this crummy old war.' I stamped my foot for the 39th time since Father and Mother had told me I was going to be packed off to my grandparents' house in the country—in South Australia, half way across the country. To grandparents I had never visited. Suddenly I knew what all the closed-door, whispered conversations between my parents meant. They were sending me away, like second-hand clothes. I wasn't even going to be home at Christmastime.

'There's no time for hysterics, Henrietta.' Mother stood in front of my wardrobe. 'You're old enough to help pack a suitcase. Daisy will be along shortly to help you, but she has her own packing to do. She's going with you.'

o0o

I'd finally overheard a conversation in the dining room. I'd been hiding under the table after every meal with no success because Mother and Father had stopped chatting over meals. That particular evening, they'd forgotten to retire to Father's study with the door firmly shut, a habit that had begun the day shots were fired in Melbourne.

Under the table, I wished I'd brought a pillow. The servants wouldn't notice. There were only two left, the cook who had become the housekeeper as well, and Daisy, who was always in a state of nervous confusion.

I don't know why I bothered, hiding and eavesdropping. Mother and Father were speaking in half sentences.

'I don't like it either, but James...'

'I know. I didn't agree with you at first.'

'And now?'

'It's probably for the best, Frances.'

'It will only be for the duration.'

The worst day of my life!

December, 1914

I couldn't believe my parents would send me away, and to Mother's parents, grandparents I hardly know. I never thought Father would agree. I don't think he would've if it hadn't been for those shots fired in Victoria, which is practically a stone's throw away according to Daisy. Poor Daisy who has to accompany me. I made Mother angry by asking if she was packing Cook off as well. She simply can't live without Mrs Brentworth.

Father drove us to Central Station, Daisy and I. It was cold. Mother kissed me quickly. I wiped the kiss away. 'It's only for the duration,' she said, then turned to give instructions to Daisy, who cried so much Mother called her a silly goose and threatened to slap her face. I didn't cry at all. I hated her, and I would hate South Australia and everything in it.

Deliberately standing with one foot over the white line at Hornsby railway station annoyed Mother but I didn't care.

'Get back here, Henrietta Eloise Parsons,' said Mother, delivering a swift slap to the platform with her umbrella to reinforce the point.

I shuffled slow feet across the platform. Daisy was a nervous wreck, showing every sign of a nervous breakdown. She clutched our tickets so tightly her hands cramped. She probably didn't want to go either but no-one else could be spared, certainly not Mother.

'You change at Central Station, Daisy.' Mother pulled her gloves on, always a sign any discussion was over. 'My father—Bill Kent will meet you in Adelaide and take you to Freeling.'

'Yes, Ma'am.' Daisy dropped her purse. 'Crikey.'

Mother flinched. According to her, Daisy was as common as muck.

o0o

I was quite wrong about Daisy. Once we were on the train she relaxed so much I worried she'd fall asleep by the time we got to Central Station and we'd miss our stop. It wouldn't matter after that because we had a shared sleeper cabin.

Once aboard the Indian Pacific, Daisy really came to life. We made numerous trips to the dining car. Daisy was a plump, cheerful girl who had a fondness for sweets. She was a great hit with the staff. I guess they didn't expect the companion of an upper class brat to be so chatty and down to earth. It turned out they thought she was my mother.

Daisy laughed at that and said she wouldn't mind as I was a dear little lamb. So the staff soon forgot my exclusive Vaucluse address, my snobby speech that I didn't know I had until it was pointed out, and treated us like one of them, or two of them.

The train carried many soldiers and Daisy flirted with them.

'Poor dears need a bit of cheering up,' she said with a wink.

At many of the stations we passed or stopped to take on more passengers, there were long lines of soldiers, all kitted out in new uniforms.

Later, I found Daisy with her head in a newspaper.

I sat down beside her. She wiped tears with a dainty lace handkerchief, a parting gift from Mother.

'So many,' she said, staring out of the train window. '50,000 of our boys, signed up. Enlisted in the blooming Australian Infantry Forces. What an abominable waste.'

Then she said sorry, smiled brightly and took me to the dining room for almond custard cake and English Breakfast tea.

o0o

Grandpapa picked us up at the station. He had a bushy moustache and twinkling eyes. He insisted on carrying my suitcase. Daisy had a young soldier look after her's.

'Suitor already, young Daisy.' Grandpapa chuckled as he led us to a buggy with two horses. 'I hope you two aren't too tired for a ride in this old thing.'

'Oh no,' I said. 'We had oodles of sleep on the train. We had beds and all.'

'Beds. Well I never. Beds on a train. What will they think of next.'

Fields of wheat in South Australia

December 1914

Grandpapa and Grandmamma were nothing like I thought they would be. They were like two friends I'd been waiting to meet all my life.

My expectations of a boring life were swiftly swept aside. The horse and buggy was a first. We clipped along at a rocking pace, through fields of wheat that had been harvested under a wide blue sky.

To my delight, my new teacher, Miss Reed, mixed up my enrolment, possibly due to Grandmamma's filling in of the forms. Grandmamma had never been impressed with me being named after the other (wrong) side of the family. At roll call Miss Reed called out Eloise Parsons. I saw a chance to leave that dreaded name, Henrietta behind. I jumped to my feet, yelling 'Here, Miss!'

This upset the girl sitting next to me, a shy girl who burst into tears. Miss Reid said there was no need to leap about the classroom like a Parisian cancan dancer and promptly moved me to the front of the classroom.

Grandpapa worked at Heinrich's corner store. He worried about everything: late milk deliveries; the noisy parrot Grandmamma had adopted; keeping children from pilfering sweets from the lolly shelf; and the war, always the war.

Grandmamma found constant talk of war irritating. So irritating she took an afternoon sherry in a nice crystal glass to put the world to rights again. According to Grandmamma, the men were making too much of the whole blasted thing. Anyone who knows anything about aviation knows that the German planes have trouble flying further than their own country, much less crossing several oceans to drop bombs in a South Australian backyard.

For the first time in my life I was surrounded by other children and Grandmamma's kitchen was full of chatter and food. Christmas seemed to go on for days, with dinner, suppers and parties, so different from Mother's.

The Duration

November, 1918

Grandpapa and Grandmamma were like two lovebirds. I was surprised to learn that Grandmamma was Austrian. Her name was Helena, and her maiden name was Walburga. She had travelled as a laundry maid on the *Kaiserin Elizabeth* on the staff of Archduke Franz Ferdinand when he visited Australia. She attended the Sydney Royal Easter Show where she met Grandpapa, William (Bill) Kent, a farmer from South Australia. What a romance!

It also meant Grandmamma was German, Grandpapa said. The government was rounding up German people because of the war with Germany.

'They are only taking the men,' Grandpapa said. 'It's different in Freeling. So many of the local farmers are German the whole country would run out of wheat and flour! And the army depends on the hay we send, as well as horses.'

The whole community supported each other, and other communities too. In nearby towns women were trying to look after farms with husbands and fathers gone, but Grandpapa said it was even worse for women in the city. The country women could at least grow their own food.

Grandmamma and Grandpapa had many wonderful friends. Mrs Frauenfelder and Grandmamma were often in the kitchen with their Austrian recipe books, as they cooked for families whose men had been taken away to camps because the government considered them possible enemies or spies, even if they'd been born in Australia.

Daisy found much to admire in country life and was thrilled when Mother said there was no need for her to return. She started helping out in Grandpapa's store, meeting people and going to dances. This gave Grandmamma more time to bake, potter in the garden and call on friends with hampers of food.

Daisy met a young farmer at the store. She was so nervous that she had to repack his order half a dozen times. Grandpapa was greatly amused, which was odd for him and he was such a worrier. 'Smitten with him, she is,' he said.

Grownups are odd creatures. Daisy had chatted easily with the soldiers on the train. I couldn't see how dropping things meant she was falling in love. But they got engaged. Daisy wrote to Mother to tell her. I thought Mother would be pleased, but she wrote and said she was disappointed Daisy wasn't returning even though she'd told Daisy she needn't bother coming back.

We sometimes went to the city. Grandmamma and Grandpapa arranged for us to have a family photograph with a Bavarian-born photographer, Paul Dubrotzki, who ran a photographic studio. We heard later he'd been arrested.

Mrs Frauenfelder said, 'It's horrible. We left Germany because of what we hated, the persecution of our people. We left! And now...They take us all away. They drink the Resch's beer, but imprison Edmund Resch—and that lovely photographer, Paul Dubotski—him they have taken to Torrens Island Camp.'

Grandmamma said—'If they take our men, they have no bread.'

Mrs Frauenfelder laughed, the sort of laugh someone has when they're trying to cheer themselves up, as well as others. 'You're living with the enemy now, little Henrietta,' she said.

That's when I knew why Mother had so little contact with her parents. She was ashamed of her German heritage.

Mr Dubrotzki was allowed to take his camera to the camp. Grandmamma and some of the other women visited him, bringing food and clothing. The camp was a horrible place, surrounded by barbed wire. I knew little of the traumas of a distant war, but was shocked by this. Not all the men were taken away. Many Freeling Germans had enlisted and gone to fight. That made things even more confusing.

I thought of the war differently then. I'd only known the stream of tobacco-smelling men in suits with their ties loosened, worried looks and newspapers. Mother's high teas for the Australian Comforts Fund, to raise money and organise everyday women to knit socks and make aid packages for the troops.

Now, the war had become about people.

o0o

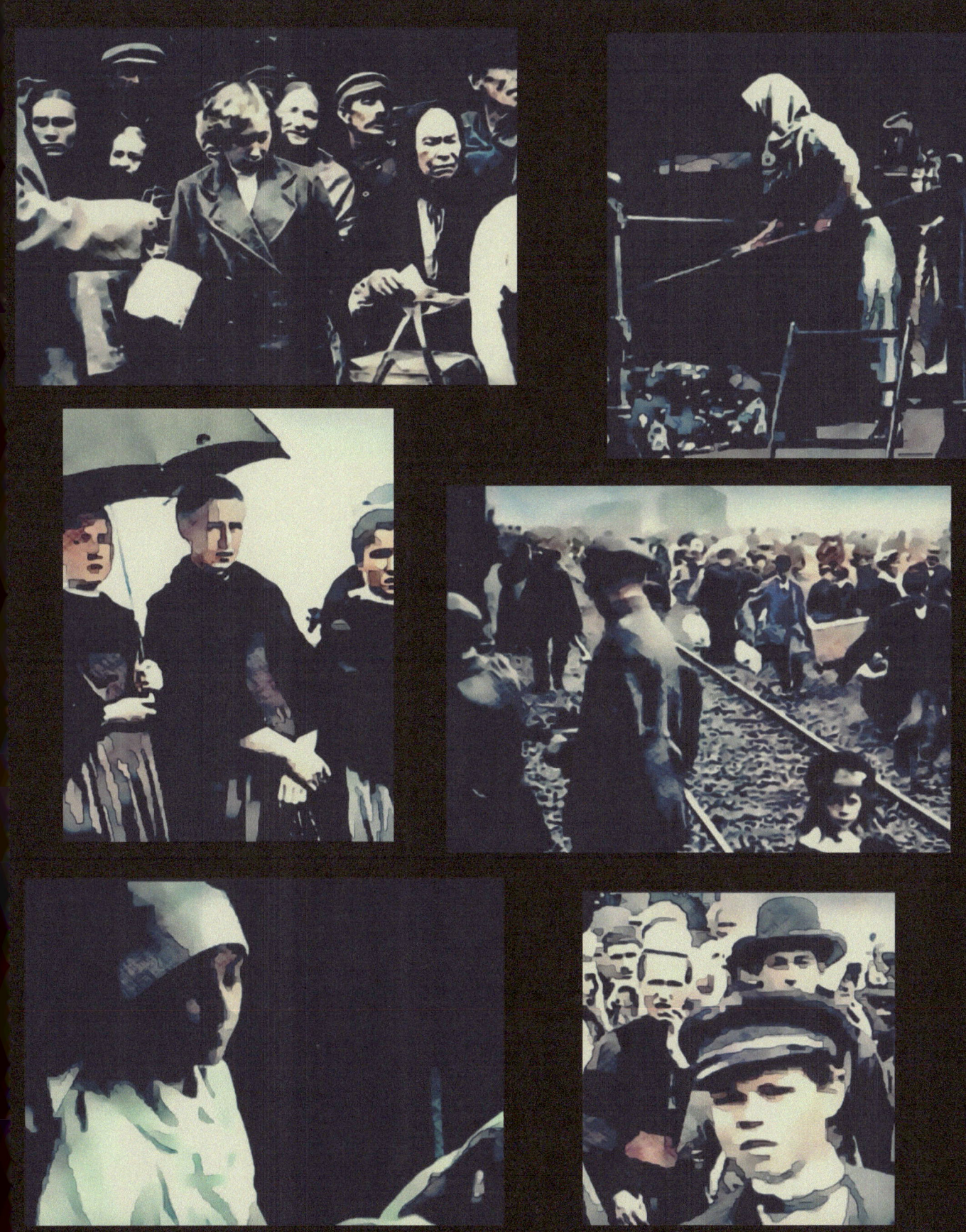

There was a boy next door my age, Peter Oldfield. His father had just shipped out as a soldier in the infantry. Peter thought war was a terrific thing. He spent a lot of time pretending to be a soldier, or a pilot.

He was fascinated with Grandpapa's latest project, building an air raid shelter in the backyard. Grandpapa was pleased when Peter and I begged to help him with the shelter, but when we brought up the subject of a suitable place in the shelter for Rebecca the Parrot and her cage, Grandpapa told us that he no longer required our assistance. So, we decided to build our own, on the quiet, of course—grownups are funny about that sort of thing.

Late one afternoon when Grandpapa was busy in the store and Grandmamma was having a nap after her sherry, we dug near the peach tree behind the garden shed. We hadn't asked just in case the grownups didn't approve so we threw an old oily tarp over it at night.

Peter and I made very slow progress with our air raid shelter. Grandmamma had warned us that Grandpapa had a very keen ear for shenanigans. I think she knew what we were up to, but said nothing. She'd been miffed that Grandpapa had said he didn't care what happened to the daft parrot. He wasn't going to share an air raid shelter with a squawking bird while bombs fell overhead.

There was a drought that first year, which couldn't be worse timing according to Grandpapa. But then he said that about a lot of things. The doctor was busy with children who had whooping cough, so I had to stay home a bit.

Father came to visit every year, which was just wonderful. Aunt Bea came twice, a double treat. I'd been busy, but not so busy that I hadn't missed home. I'd even missed Father smelly cigars. He said Mother didn't come because she found the heat in tolerable. The next time he visited he said she found the cold intolerable. I began to understand the sad look in Grandmamma's eyes whenever Mother was mentioned.

Father went all over the place with Grandpapa. He found our air raid shelter hole and I told a terrible lie and said Peter and I were digging a veggie patch to help out with the war effort. Luckily, Father said nothing to Grandpapa.

Disaster struck Peter and I. The butcher's dog, Caesar Augustus, fell in our air raid shelter hole. The dog set up a racket barking and whimpering. It wouldn't have been so bad but it happened in the middle of the night. Which meant that Grandpapa had to get up in his nightshirt and rescue 'the poor mutt'.

Grandpapa was terribly embarrassed. He had to get dressed and get the buggy out, even though Grandmamma said he could bring the dog inside by the fire and things could wait until morning. Grandpapa said that was a poor-spirited idea and he'd never be able to look the butcher in the eye again if he hadn't sorted his dog immediately. He made me go with him to apologise and explain. I got the story so tangled that I was about to burst into tears when Mr Frantz laughed and gave me a biscuit. Grandpapa said there was no need to reward the stupid act of a couple of silly kids.

'I should have had the wretched dog in the yard,' said Mr Frantz. 'Don't be too hard on the girl, Bill. Here, have a biscuit yourself – sit down now that you're here. I have a lovely single malt.'

'Don't mind if I do.' Grandpapa sat down.

Peter was glad he hadn't been woken in the middle of the night to apologise to Mr Frantz, but changed his mind when he found out I'd had a plate of biscuits.

o0o

Then, things changed. The war seemed endless. Horrible stories were being told by the soldiers who'd been sent home wounded. These stories were whispered, especially around us kids. Telegrams started to arrive and families were shocked and grieving. People stopped looking forward to the post arriving. Any day they might hear of a son or father, missing, wounded or dead.

Daisy told her fella that she wouldn't marry him until the war was over. She wasn't going to marry someone who'd race off overseas to fight the minute the ink dried on the marriage license.

One day in 2015, Peter's mum got a yellow telegram. Peter's father had been horribly wounded at Gallipoli and had been taken to England.

Peter threw all his war toys into the hole we dug, set them on fire, then buried them there. Grandpapa stood there with him, a hand on his shoulder and helped him fill in the hole.

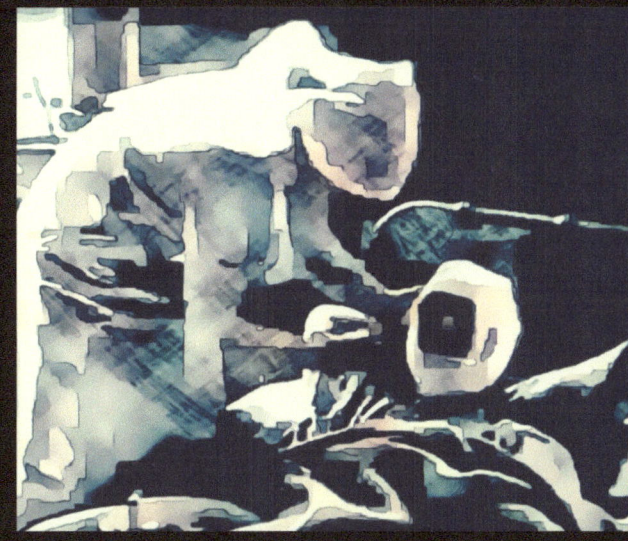

Armistice

November, 1918

I could have gone home as soon as Germany signed a document called the Armistice. They signed it on the 11th hour of the 11th day of the 11th month.

I'd seen Father and missed home less and less. I'd made new friends and found a life that made Vaucluse, high teas and chandeliers seem different than I'd thought of them before. I was 13 and would start high school the following year. Some fancy grammar school I supposed. Mother wrote of all the delights that awaited me. Somehow they didn't measure up to life with my grandparents in Freeling.

I made Daisy's wedding an excuse to stay until the New Year. I'd wanted another Christmas, another picnic, a bit longer with a house that welcomed friends all year long, day and night, come as you are.

The landscape of wheat fields and haystacks faded and ebbed into the snarl and snap of traffic. Grandpapa and Grandmamma insisted on taking me to the station for my return to Sydney. I felt sad leaving the vast land and endless blue skies. I'd been angry when I left Sydney, but on the return journey I cried like a baby. I thought I'd only be in Freeling for a few months. It had been four years.

Back in Vaucluse, Mother seemed intent on making up for lost time. Maybe trying to cover her guilt at not visiting. She organised a party with all my old friends, most of whom were awkward around me. I insisted she invite Aunt Bea.

Aunt Bea arrived looking glamorous with an American marine on her arm. He was a negro and Mother was shocked and rude to Aunt Bea. I was so angry with her that I spent the next week speaking German, something that irritated Mother far more than Aunt Bea's boyfriend.

I'd done a lot of growing up. There was so much about me that Mother didn't know and I would never be the same again.

oOo

Afterword

Some authors write very clever afterwords or get other very clever people to write them. This afterword is different. It's my version of the history of the war. At school we were told of the glory and sacrifice, and the inevitability of war. All that was true enough in its own way, but the history books left a whole lot of stuff out. Like how lots of the soldiers became ill from terrible diseases that affected their minds and bodies.

The soldiers who lay dead on the fields of war were not the only victims. Many others were broken, never to recover. The recording and telling of history is changing. Historians now talk about the cold, the hunger, the lack of medical aid, the everyday problems of the soldiers, the mud, the crazy waiting for the enemy to appear, the boredom, the horror in the trenches. And so much more...

In the First World War much of the world was involved in the fight, on one side or the other. And the silliest thing of all is that the crown heads, King George V of England, Kaiser Wilhelm of Germany and Tsar Nicholas of Russia were cousins, grandsons of Queen Victoria of England. Even though the soldiers who fought their way across Europe had never met, the men that wore the crowns in those three countries had been photographed together for the family album often, even spent Christmases together.

It's all very confusing. And it's even more confusing when you try to look at a map and work out what was happening because countries were always nipping off bits of other countries and adding them to their Empires. And basically that's the reason the whole thing started.

Rulers of countries never seemed to understand they could invade countries and take resources like spices, or coal, or oil; they could tell the people that they belonged to a great empire, but they could never buy the loyalty of the people no matter how brutal or persuasive their actions.

Not for long anyway.

The story of the First World War begins on a street in Sarajevo, the capital city of Bosnia. Archduke Franz Ferdinand of Austria, heir to the throne of Austria-Hungary, was shot and killed by Gavrilo Princip, a Serbian rebel on 28 June 1914. Princip was part of a militant group called the Black Hand, a group that was angry about Austria taking over Bosnia, which had been a Serbian state.

Franz Ferdinand's uncle, Archduke Franz Joseph was furious about the attack. He sent an ultimatum to Serbia—'let Austrian authorities into Serbia to investigate the assassination, giving a deadline in a month's time. Or else.'

King Peter I, the ruler of Serbia, knew what "or else" meant. It meant if you don't let us, we'll invade your country—there's no worse trouble to be in. King Peter was from the Karađorđević dynasty—a word you don't want to try to say in public until you've had a lot of practice. Royalty in Serbia was unstable, past kings had been exiled, deposed, assassinated and ousted. In spite of that, the Serbians refused to give in to Austria's demands. So when the deadline was up Austria-Hungary declared war on Serbia, and attacked. The Serbians fought with everything they had, but lost. They lost so badly a quarter of the population had been killed by the end of the WWI, and like many other countries after WWI, royalty was finished. There would be no more kings.

Russia had a pact with Serbia and attacked Germany. Germany had a pact with Austria-Hungary so they declared war on Serbia and Russia. But they'd had their eye on France and thought they might as well settle old scores while everyone was firing cannons and shooting. Germany set out to attack France. Belgium stood in the way so the German-Austrian army invaded Belgium. Belgium had a pact with England, so England declared war on Germany, Austria-Hungary and any other country that might join the other side.

Italy was a bit undecided at first, then sided with England, Russia and France. Germany visited the Turks who were in the south, put on their best manners, sent their most important people and convinced the Turks to join them.

Then both sides called on their colonies to come to their aid.

Colonies were pieces of other countries that had been "taken over" or "discovered" without bothering about the people living there.

The colonies did what they were asked and went to war. Countries like Australia, New Zealand and Canada. Then there was India, and the African colonies. None of whom felt one way or the other about the Germans, French or Europeans, other than being told they were "on the other side".

America wasn't very interested in jumping into a war on the other side of the world, and said so. America had been a colony of the British Empire as it was once called. England had sent their prisoners there, convicts they couldn't fit in their jails because they arrested people for the silliest offences and sentenced them to "exile for the term of their natural lives". But the Americans had fought the British, thrown their tea into the sea, and claimed the place for themselves.

Then the British sent their convicts to Australia, a place they claimed they'd discovered even though the whole place was already settled by Indigenous Australians. They'd landed their ships, said the place was deserted and set up camp. Then they decided to do the place up, make it more to their liking, in fact, just like England.

Australia, still being a colony, didn't have much choice about going to war After all, who would come to Australia's aid if anyone attacked? Even though Australia is bigger than Europe there's a whole lot of country that's not good for much but saltbush, frill-necked lizards and flies. Australia declared war on England's enemies, whoever they might turn out to be, and sent country lads and city boys in uniforms to wage war.

At the end of WWI, England was pretty much the only country where the monarchy remained. Kaiser Wilhelm of Germany was exiled. Tsar Nicholas was shot and killed, along with all of his family. Empire would never be the same around the world. In the aftermath, it wasn't only rulers who lost power over their own people, but many of their colonies demanded independence for their countries and they were prepared to resist, or fight. Kings, Queens, Tsars, Archdukes and Kaisers had invaded many other countries, and the people weren't going to take it any more.

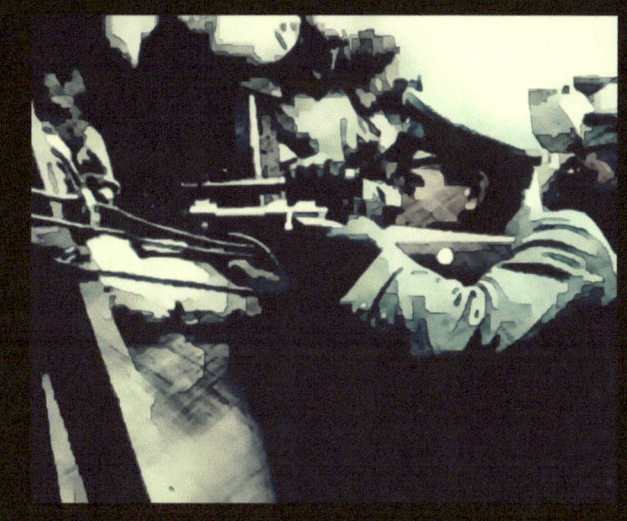

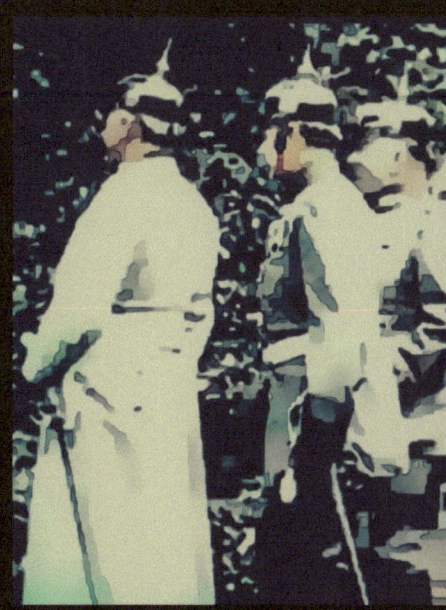

Empire—Kings, Queens, Tsars and Kaisers:
The first kings of the dynasties didn't start out as kings. They were warriors, usually invaders. Warriors that defeated lots of enemies made themselves kings. Then after a few generations everyone forgot that they'd just been an ordinary anybody to start with. People started believing that there was such a thing as royal blood, which is such a load of nonsense it's a wonder anyone fell for it. But because they'd saved the people from some dreadful threat, or said they had, the people were grateful. At least for a while. Until they realised the king had the best of everything while they went hungry and word got around that the king had created the threat in the first place by stealing land, people and resources, which meant that Kings were often defending the country from people that he and his army had smacked around in the first place. This made the common people angry. They revolted against the way the kings used their power with injustice, taking land and money, and demanding taxes that meant the people went hungry. In some countries, ordinary people weren't allowed to own land and their profits and food from farming went to the king. People started grouping together and planning revolutions to rid themselves of this kind of rule.

Invading: otherwise known as colonisation.
Invading other countries was popular, and had been for a long time, probably forever. It seemed like every second country was invading another one. This invading was also called Adding to The Empire, or "colonising" with the added load of rubbish that they were only doing it for the benefit of the people in those countries. Words like civilising and converting were also used a lot. This is called propaganda—a fancy political word for a bunch of lies designed to persuade people to think another way, see the world differently.

Invading a country meant not only taking land and resources it meant dominating the place and the people. Every country had a resistance movement with brave men and women who fought behind the scenes and protected other people who were considered enemies.

However, it was much easier to invade a place than to occupy it—a place with real people who had no say at all. And that's the secret to History. It seems like the driest, most boring subject on earth, until you understand that it's really about people like you and me.

Freeling RSL 2018

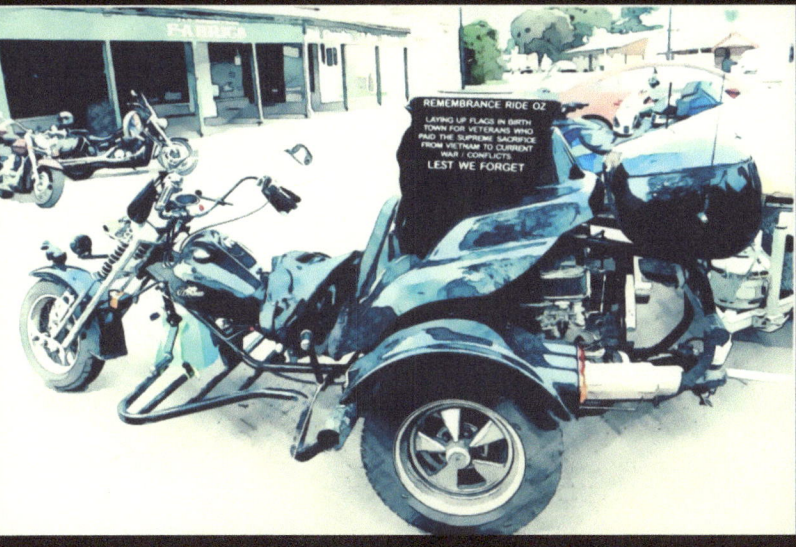

www.ingramcontent.com/pod-product-compliance
Lightning Source LLC
Chambersburg PA
CBHW042142290426
44110CB00002B/92